Aquarium plants

does not set out to be a complete work on plants which are suitable for aquariums but describes a variety of attractive plants, and gives details of their origin and growth characteristics plus sound advice on the layout and decoration of Tropical Aquariums.

The author, an enthusiastic aquarist for many years writes in an informative and readable style and shows how plants can form an attractive setting which will display your fish to their best advantage. The text is illustrated with line drawings both of plants and tank layouts.

Aquarium Plants and Decoration

R.F. O'Connell

Great Outdoors Publishing Co

Great Outdoors Publishing Co
4747 25th Street North
St. Petersburg
Florida 33714

SBN 8200—0112—0

Library of Congress
Number 78-139109

Printed in Great Britain.

<u>Author's Note</u>.

Certain plants are illustrated but not described, these plants in the Authors opinion are not suited for home aquaria.

They are sometimes offered for sale and are therefore included for ease of identification.

R.F. O'Connell

Layout

Much of the visual appeal of a well planned aquarium is provided by the plants and depends to a large extent on the manner in which they are arranged. Plants, together with natural pieces of rock, and other decorative devices will present a background to show off the fish to their best advantage. Plants also play an important part in the general function of the small, compact world contained within the glass walls of the aquarium.

The function of plants should not be given an exaggerated importance, biologically fish, will survive and remain healthy in aquariums which are entirely devoid of plantlife providing alternative measures are taken to create aeration and to remove any waste products, but a tank devoid of vegetation is like a room without furniture — empty and uninviting. After all, the fact that underwater plants are growing successfully in your drawing room makes them objects of interest in themselves, apart from their decorative and useful function.

The usual function provided by the plants is the assimilation of carbon dioxide given off by the fish, and the release of oxygen into the water. This process is known as photosynthesis and only takes place under the stimulus of strong light, and requires water and the greenness (chlorophyll) incorporated in the plants. Naturally some types of plants are more efficient from the aquarist's viewpoint, than others, and many plants, e.g. *Vallisneria* produce oxygen so abundantly that it can be seen leaving the leaves as a slow thin, stream of tiny pearl-like bubbles.

Aquatic plants are nourished principally by various dissolved salts including nitrogen in the form of ammonia and nitrate; phosphate; potassium, and lesser quantities of calcium, magnesium, iron, sulphate, copper, cobalt, manganese, boron, and molybdenum, they also require a few other trace elements and carbon dioxide. Some of the plant nutrients are found in natural waters, whilst others are provided by the gradual mineralization of organic matter. This organic matter is provided by the excreta from the fish initially and the subsequent action of micro-organisms. Therefore, it is obvious that the fish play their part in maintaining the plant life, whilst the plants offer a service in return.

Plants will thrive in an aquarium devoid of fish, but it will then become necessary to provide the necessary nutrient from some other source.

It is rarely, if ever, necessary to use anything other than aquarium sand or gravel as a planting medium, but if the aquarist has an inventive turn of mind, and feels he must experiment, then he should do so by all means. *Garden soil,* should never by used as it contains too many substances that are likely to give rise to trouble in time. It also takes a long time to settle and is easily disturbed.

The planting media, or bottom soil, has been a much discussed subject over the years, but no general agreement has been reached to indicate the best, all round, media. One suggestion is that the floor of the aquarium should be spread with an initial layer of clay bearing sand, and then covered by another layer of clean, washed gravel. Other suggestions include an under-layer of peat, or potting compost, and the local injection of fertilizers made from pulverised sheep manure, or even the pellet droppings of rabbits and guinea pigs, inserted into the sand, local to the plant roots. Frankly all these devices are best ignored. In a well set up aquarium the fish will supply the necessary plant nutrient in greater quantities than the plants require, and the risk of contaminating the water will not be increased by the addition of undesirable chemical and biological elements.

Never put newly acquired plants straight into an established aquarium. They should be examined first for any unwanted snails and the jelly-like adhesions of eggs, which should then be removed. Next remove any yellow or decaying leaves and rinse the plants under the tap. They should then be immersed in a solution of concentrated lime water diluted with fresh water to a proportion of six parts fresh water to one part lime water. The plants may be left in this solution for about 10 minutes, no more, and then placed in a solution of permanganate of potash for a similar period. The strenth of the potash should be a quarter grain to a gallon of water. To make the lime water, mix liberally hydrated lime in water, and let the sediment settle, then syphon off the clear water and mix as previously described.

Plants should never be allowed to become dry during transit, or at any other time for that matter. They should be wrapped in several layers of newspaper soaked in water with a final wrapping of greaseproof to prevent evaporation.

When adding plants to a filled tank, a pair of planting sticks may prove helpful. The plant can be pushed into the position with one stick whilst the other is used to heap the sand around the roots. The sticks can be made from any thin strips of wood sand-papered smooth, split bamboo is ideal. A 'V' notch in the end of one will allow stray root strands to be pushed under the sand.

If the plants are not firmly anchored into the sand their buoyancy will cause them to rise to the surface, but once they establish their root patterns this problem will not arise. Plants with small roots can be anchored temporarily with thin strips of lead wound around their base, but the lead should not be squeezed so hard that it bruises or injures the delicate structure of the plant. If the roots become black through contact with the lead, or for any other reason, you can restore them to their natural colour by floating them in water exposed to strong sunlight for 24 hours.

Plants should never be bunched too closely together. They should be planted so as to allow water and light to reach the stems. Another disadvantage of closely packed roots is that they form sediment traps, and may encourage the growth of unwanted bacteria.

Plants that form runners from the roots should not be planted too close to other plants as they will need space to spread their roots *Vallisneria* and similar types should never have their crowns buried in the sand. The diagrams show the correct method of planting. Root filaments should always hang down and be planted vertically into the depression made for them in the sand, the tips should never be bent upwards. Finally, remember that *all* your plants will need to receive light so plan your layout so that the small plants are not overshadowed by the larger ones.

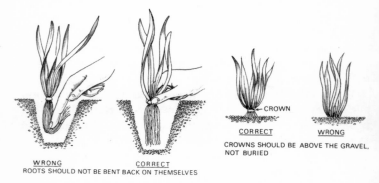

CROWN

CORRECT   WRONG

CROWNS SHOULD BE ABOVE THE GRAVEL, NOT BURIED

WRONG   CORRECT
ROOTS SHOULD NOT BE BENT BACK ON THEMSELVES

Diagrams showing method of planting roots.

The layout, or the method of furnishing an aquarium will, of course, be governed mostly by personal taste and artistic ability, but before the aquarium is planted, or even filled with water, consideration should be given to the site chosen for the tank. Only too often the aquarium is sited initially in a particular position for no other reason than there happens to be a convenient space in the room, subsequent considerations may well decide that a totally different position is more suitable to the room decor, and an aquarium full of water is not re-sited easily – it must be emptied before it can be moved. The inclusion of aquaria as a furnishing media, not only increases the pleasure of the hobbyist because he can observe the behaviour of his fish in the comfort of his home, but also has the added advantage of enhancing the decor of a room or hallway and provides an animated scene that can be enjoyed by the whole family.

Firstly, always try to install one or two electrical plug points adjacent to the tank; this will enable the wires for heaters and any other electrical operated equipment to be either concealed entirely, or neatly run under a shelf or along a skirting board.

Air-lifts and outside filters can detract from the rectangular presentation of the tank if simply hung on the frame in a haphazard manner. Endeavour, therefore, to conceal such equipment with a frame or board incorporated in the furnishing, unsightly tubing and connectors can be concealed in the same manner.

Fig. 1.

Fig. 1 shows a relatively simple, but effective presentation for a row of tanks, requiring nothing more than a *strong* one piece, or multi-base stand. This arrangement fits well into the modern home, with the suspended strip lighting giving illumination both to the aquaria and the room.

Fig. 2.

Another modern impression is shown in Fig. 2, the 'ladder' type frame supporting the tank must be strong enough to support the heavy water-filled aquarium.

Fig. 3 shows a television stand adapted to take an aquarium, but this suggestion is only intended for small tanks.

Fig. 4 is a more ambitious scheme intended for large rooms and large aquaria. The base for practical purposes,

Acorus gramineus
foliis variegatis (left)
Acorus gramineus (right)

Anubias lanceolata

Fig. 3.

Fig. 4.

must be firm and able to support the considerable weight of such a large aquarium. Brickwork is ideal for this purpose, and can be styled to the general decorative scheme.

An easily made corner layout.

These suggested plans for combining decor and aquariums are by no means exhaustive, they are intended simply to indicate a few basic approaches to the subject, the arrangements are limited only by the purse and inventiveness of the aquarist.

Having decided upon the site for the aquarium and made certain that it is firm and does not rock on its support, we can turn our attention to the arrangement of the plants. How you approach this particular aspect of fishkeeping is, as previously stated, very much a matter of personal taste, but it is not unreasonable to assume that the majority of aquarists will want to combine an attractive appearance with a natural-looking underwater landscape.

First cover the floor of the aquarium with about a two inch layer of thoroughly washed aquarium gravel. This can be levelled or contoured. If using an under-gravel filter, it is an advantage to have the gravel more or less the same depth all over. Contours in the gravel will subside once the aquarium has been filled with water, unless some support is provided. One method is to use thoroughly cleaned stones of various sizes. The diagrams show how this can be achieved, as otherwise the water-saturated gravel will soon find its own level. As an example, assume it is required to make one corner of the floor of the aquarium higher than the general level, or to provide a gentle slope from the front to the back, then place large stones along the back, smaller ones in front of these and so on. Then fill in the spaces between the stones with gravel and finally cover the whole floor with a final layer of gravel. It is important to ensure that the stones have been cleaned thoroughly in water, and any dirt removed with a stiff brush, finally they should boiled in water for about 10 minutes to ensure that they are germ free.

Rocks used to support tiers of gravel.

Remember to provide adequate pockets of gravel in which to set the plants, and do not use any more stones than is necessary to provide the desired effect. Another method commonly used to create slopes is to insert strips of clear plastic into the gravel to form barriers which hold the gravel in tiers.

The most effective and natural looking tank arrangement that can be used either with or without under-gravel filters, is to first provide a level gravel base about two inches deep and then lay thin pieces of flat Devon, or similar rock, diagonally across one rear corner to form a wall and then fill in behind the wall with gravel. Very natural layouts can be effected using this method and a little imagination and it has the additional advantage of leaving practically the whole of the gravel free to accept the plant roots.

Tank layout.

When selecting rocks remember that your aquarium should represent, as near as possible, a natural cross-section of underwater terrain. Multi-shaped rocks and rocks varying considerably in colour should never be put in the same tank, they are unlikely to be found together naturally. Apart from providing banks of gravel at varying levels, rocks can be used to form terraces, and arches. It is not essential to install any rockwork, as plants alone could be used to provide very attractive arrangements.

Two favourite rocks used by aquarists are Cumberland stone and the green-brown flat, slaty rocks found in Devonshire streams. These flat natural pieces of rock can be pressed into the gravel to form pinnacles, or laid flat and built up, one upon the other, to form natural looking ledges.

Interesting slopes.

Well weathered pieces are the best, but avoid pieces with jagged edges or protrusions which may injure your fish. The types of rocks suitable for aquarium decoration must be insoluble. Avoid using rocks of a soft or synthetic nature, as these tend to break up after prolonged immersion. If you have a doubtful piece of rock, put it in a bucket of clean water for a few days, if an oily ring appears on the surface, do not use it.

In the interest of hygiene it is advisable to avoid nooks and crannies in the rockwork that can harbour uneaten food, this will pollute the water and provide sediment traps. They could also hide a dead fish which could also cause water pollution. After the rocks have been sited to your liking, press them into the gravel, then if there are any pockets anywhere, fill them in with gravel.

It is possible to fashion your own rockwork using sand and cement, but it is not an advisable practice. However, it can be done. After the rocks have been moulded into the desired shapes and due care taken to ensure that no sharp projections have been left, leave for about a week for the cement to harden, then boil for at least an hour in clean water to remove most of the free lime. Next soak the 'rock' in a strong solution of permanganate of potash for about six hours. In addition to disinfecting the rock this also adds to its attractiveness by giving it a natural weathered appearance. After a final soak under a running tap for about an hour the rock is ready for use.

A very good design.

The next stage is to add the plants. Avoid moulding the overall design of the interior so that the result is completely symmetrical, a plant or rock placed in the centre of the tank with equal numbers of identical plant on each side is a sorry sight and will certainly not look very natural, neither will an aquarium with all the weight' tucked into one corner without any balancing piece. The aim should be to provide a well balanced scheme with tall plants at the back and the smaller and daintier specimens to the fore, keep an eye on proportion. The aquarium should look well balanced. Remember that the use of excessively large rocks will have the effect of reducing the impression of depth, and do not scatter the plants around in a haphazard manner, as this will result in an untidy and unnatural design, it is much better to group the various species.

Ideal for two or three fish.

Many aquarist supply stores carry a wide range of plastic plants, some of which are quite excellent artifices, personally, I see no virtue in using these plants in a fresh water tank when one can see the real thing, however, tastes differ, and the odd sprig may well be used to advantage if used with discretion. Plastic tree trunks can be used to hide filters and other apparatus and are effective when reproducing the terrain of tropical rain forest rivers.

The numbers of plants one should use is somewhat arbitary, in one sense the more the merrier, but if the aquarium is too crowded with plants, the fish cannot be seen, therefore, the following suggestions are average requirements for a tank measuring 24″ × 12″ × 12″

18 Sagittaria	about 12 inches long.
Cabomba	about 12 inches long.
8 Myriophyllum	about 12 inches long.

or

18	Vallisneria	about 12 inches long.
2	Indian Fern	Large
1	Amazon Sword	Medium
6	Ambulia	Medium.

Hair grass and other small decorative plants can be added for effect.

The inclusion of gnarled branches and twisted roots is most effective, but they can have some effect on the condition of the water by releasing organic acids from the wood. The only really safe woods to use are those that have lain in water for a number of years and have a petrified appearance, it is advisable to further cleanse these branches by washing for an extended period in a clean stream or lake, followed by boiling in salt water, and further washing in clean water for about a two week period. Finally boil in clean water before actually putting them into aquarium.

An effective use of twigs etc.

Even after taking all these precautions, there is no guarantee that their inclusion will not turn the water cloudy by releasing certain mineral compounds.

Under no circumstances use fresh branches or roots. These release decomposable substances into the water which can cause pollution, which is harmful to the fish.

One final word on layout — whatever objects you put into your aquarium always ensure they are clean, free from dirt, have no hidden crevices to hold substances which could cause pollution and that they have been thoroughly disinfected as previously described.

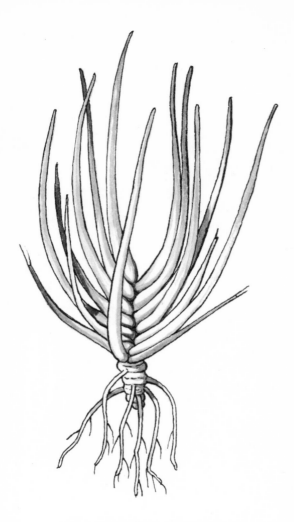

Acorus calamus angustifolius

Commonly known as the Sweet Flag, this plant can be grown submerged, but it is more suited to the margins of ponds. Propagates by cuttings of the rhizome, and should be planted in a medium containing clay and peat.

Plants

Acorus gramineus (Japanese Rush)

This pretty little plant is found naturally in the calm waters of East Asia, where it grows in swampy terrain, sometimes partly submerged, sometimes completely on dry land, but in the aquarium it grows totally submerged.

A. gramineus is a small, very attractive little plant, rarely exceeding a few inches in height; therefore, it is an ideal decorative piece to use near the front of the tank. It is decidedly rush-like with narrow, grass-like, pointed leaves, that sprout direct from the rootstock, their colour is bright to dark green.

This particular plant may well be described as *A. pusillis*, *A. japonicus*, or *A. intermedius*, they are not however, different species, but simply varieties of *A. gramineus.*

This is not a difficult plant to grow providing it is maintained in a moderate temperature, it does not like very warm water.

Propagates by splitting the rootstock, but because this species does not root very fast it is necessary to anchor with strips of lead, or with glass rods.

A. calamus is a similar species growing somewhat taller, but it is not suitable for tropical aquariums.

Acorus calamus variegatis

This plant is a variegated form of *A. calamus*, and like *A. calamus* it is not really suited to the aquarium although it is sometimes sold for the purpose.

Anubias congensis

This is another species that is only partially successful in the aquarium. Young plants in deep, sandy loam, and maintained at a temperature not lower than 25°C, will grow more or less successfully but it is best suited to the conditions of a moist vivarium.

Anubias lanceolata

This is a very attractive plant with its lanceolate leaves exhibiting minute cross-veining. Although reputed to thrive in moist soil in shady places, it is not particularly suited to the aquarium. A similar species, *A. nana*, is much better suited to the home aquarium.

Aponogeton fenestralis (Madagascar Lace Plant)

This plant comes from the Island of Madagascar and has been a firm favourite among aquarists for a number of years, but it is not an very easy plant to grow.

It is the leaf structure that makes this plant so unusual, the tissues between the nervures, and veins is always absent giving the leaves the appearance of fine lace, hence its popular name. The leaves are oval, and slightly pointed at the base and the tip, they can grow to 12 inches long and 3 inches wide. The rootstock is cylindrical.

A. fenestralis is not an easy plant to cultivate in the aquarium, it requires soft slightly acid water, and a weak or diffused light. The open lattice structure of the leaves collect algae very readily and this chokes the plant and stunts its growth.

Propagates by runners which can be divided from the rootstock as soon as they reach 1 inch in length.

Aponogeton ulvaceus

Found naturally in Madagascar, this plant is one of the larger plants available to aquarist. The leaves are a very delicate light green in colour and may well reach a length of 12 inches and a width up to 3 inches. The attractiveness of the plant is enhanced by the wavy edges to the leaves.

Because of their large size these plants require a spacious aquarium, they also thrive best in a water temperature around 75°F (24°C) in summer, and a little less in winter.

A. ulvaceus is not a particular difficult species to cultivate but they can prove frustrating to aquarists not particularly skilled in plant culture. Like *A. fenestralis* it prefers soft slightly acid water and the leaf surfaces kept free of algae and settled mulm.

Propagates by seeds and runners.

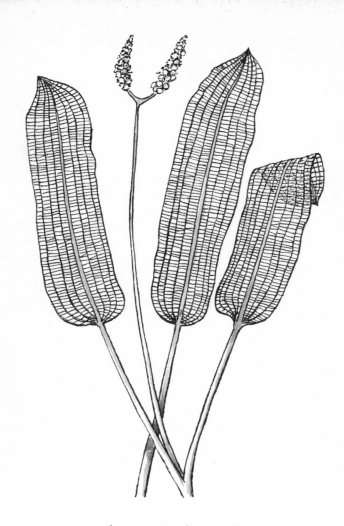

Aponogeton fenestralis

These are most attractive, ornamental, showy plants requiring some skill by the aquarist for their successful cultivation. They require soft lighting, and very soft, slightly acid water. A mantle of duckweed or viceia on the surface of the water will provide a natural screen to soften the light (see text).

Aponogeton undulatus

Aponogeton ulvaceus

Ceratophyllum demersum
Hornwort

Ceratopteris thalictroides

Aponogeton undulatus

This species is an ideal plant for the smaller aquaria, the plant only growing to about 9 inches tall. The leaves are a beautiful brilliant green, tapering to a point at the tips, and more rounded at the base. The leaf edges are slightly crinkled like the edges of torn paper. The actual leaf rarely exceeds 12 inches in length or 2 inches wide.

This is not a fast growing plant and rarely flowers in the aquarium.

A. undulatus offered by most stockists is generally a species cross-bred with *A. crispus*. It is an attractive little species nevertheless.

Azolla caroliniana (Fairy Moss)

Normally found in the tropical and sub-tropical zones of America, and Southern Europe where it was subsequently introduced. This rather unusual floating plant is composed of very small sage green leaves overlapping one another like the scales on a fish, or tiles on a roof. On the underside of the leaves many long thread-like root strands hang down in the water. When used in an indoor aquarium, they should be spread thinly otherwise they will shadow the other plants below. Under natural conditions Azolla thrives well in moist, warm air, under the open sky with plenty of bright light, unfortunately it does not do so well in the aquarium, it tends to wither very easily and rarely survives the winter.

Bacopa amplexicaulis

B. amplexicaulis is a species of swamp plant found naturally in Southern and Central U.S.A. It is a hardy plant with stiff stems which are somewhat brittle, consequently they are easily broken. The leaves are attached to the stem in pairs, one leaf opposite the other, and they are a beautiful

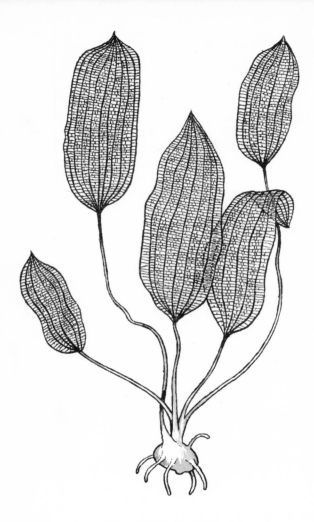

Aponogeton henkelianus

This species is similar to *A. fenestralis* except that the lacey structure of the leaves are more delicate. Cultivation requirements the same as for *A. fenestralis*.

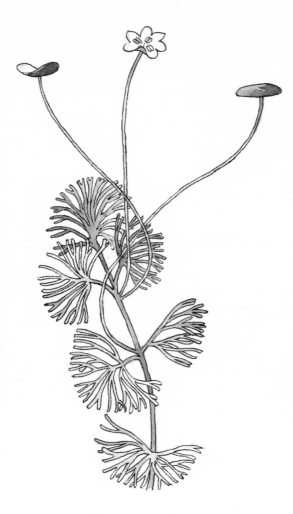

Cabomba caroliniana

This plant is not a particularly good oxygenator, neither is it very hardy. It is however very decorative and should be considered only for this purpose. *C. cairolinana rosaefolia* is a rosy red variety that can be used to contrast the greenness of other plants (see text).

shiny green, and rounded in shape. The stem is finely fluted and covered with fine hairs.

When in bloom the pretty blue to violet flowers appear in the angles of the leaves, but this plant will not bloom in the aquarium where it is totally submerged, The flowers only appear on emerged plants.

B. amplexicaulis does not like very high temperature, ideally, the temperature should be maintained at about 64°-68°F (18°-20°C) Temperatures above this level cause the plant to degenerate.

Because the plant refuses to bloom in the aquarium, and so provide seeds, propagation is effected by cuttings.

Bacopa monniera

This species is found naturally in America, Australia, Asia, Africa and possibly in Southern Europe. It is very similar to *B. amplexicaulis* with the exception of the stems and leaves which are devoid of hairs, also the leaves are slightly smaller. It is just as hardy, and has the advantage of tolerating slightly warmer water, consequently it is the better of the two mentoined species for inclusion in a tropical aquarium. Because the plant only blooms when emerged, seeds are unlikely to develop in aquarium specimen, but they can be propagated by carefully selected cuttings.

Cabomba caroliniana (Fan-Wort)

This is a very attractive plant with its leaves of delicate light green which fan out from the main stem. The fan-like leaves form an excellent retreat for young fish, but it is not considered a good spawning plant because the leaves are not sufficiently dense.

Cabomba is one of the few plants that can be bunched, but not too tightly. When purchased these plants are often tied in small bundles with a thin strip of lead, if this is so, the

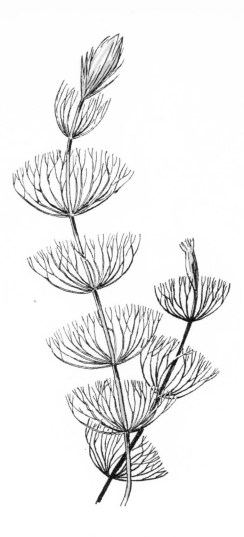

Ceratophyllum submersum

A pretty, delicate plant with light green leaves that has unfortunately brittle stems that break easily. It is best to plant a number of sprigs together, as it makes very little roots, sometimes none at all. Requires strong illumination.

Ceratoptris thalictroides

Given the correct conditions, of warmth and light, this plant can grow profusely. Its fern-like quality makes it an ideal plant for the underwater scene and for accenting a particular feature of the layout (see text).

ends should be broken off before planting into the gravel, this will give the stems a better chance to take root. It is also advisable to strip back the leaves for about 2 inches from the bottom of the stem to ensure that no leaves are buried in the gravel to become a potential source of decay.

This is not a particularly hardy plant neither is it a very good oxygenator, therefore, it is best to consider it as a decorative plant only.

Propagates by cutting.

Ceratophyllum demersum (Coarse Horn Wort)

C. demersum is a species that is found over the major parts of the world, and could become an exhibit in almost every aquarium, unfortunately it has two main drawbacks. The leaves are so brittle that they snap off at the slightest touch, and it has no real roots.

The leaves resemble *Myriophyllum* in structure except that they are coarser and are equipped with tiny thorns. It is not one of the best plants for exhibition purposes, but it is useful for breeding if it is weighted down with small pieces of lead.

If left floating in an aquarium, thin tendril like shoots grow from the stem towards the gravel in an attempt to root.

Propogates by cuttings.

C. submersum is a less common species very similar to *C. demersum* except that the leaves are thinner and more delicate.

Ceratopteris thalictroides (Indian Fern)

Found practically all over the tropic regions of the world, *C. thalictroides* was first introduced as an aquarium plant in the 1930's and since then has become an established favourite. The leaf formation is not unlike those of the chrysanthemum, with deeply indented edges, they are soft and a delicate light green in colour. The stems are rather brittle and

Crassula aquatica

This is rather a rare species that is not usually found in aquariums because it requires skilful handling, and it is only suitable for unheated tanks with very strong illumination.

rise from a compact root stock.

If planted in deep water, the stems may well reach a height of a few feet, in shallow water the leaves will either float just below the surface, or extend themselves above the surface and bear a fine cluster of rather coarse foliage.

This plant will grow readily under the stimulus of artificial light, and generally it is the best way to grow it.

It is advisable to replace old plants occasionally with younger ones as the old plants will turn brown and decay. Snails find them an appetising meal so if snails are present, it will become necessary to replace the plant at fairly frequent intervals.

For propagation *C. thalictroides* develop a perfect miniature of itself among the foliage. These miniatures then detach themselves and float to the surface. This, however, does not generally occur until part of the leaf or frond has turned brown and withered away.

Cryptocoryne (Water Trumpet)

The *Cryptocorynes* are individualist in aquatic plants. The beautiful shaped leaves have a particular character that is all their own. They are found widely distributed over South East Asia and some 46 species are known, but these are not all suitable or obtainable for aquarist.

The *Cryptocorynes* are not lovers of strong light, so if the aquarium is positioned in the shade, these are the plants to use, but it is as well to remember that they do require some light stimulus so do not overdo the shade. Because the quantity of light required by *Cryptocorynes* is less than that required by most aquatic plants, it is obviously better to group plants of this nature in a single tank otherwise a compromise must be made between the supply of strong light for some plants and a weaker light for others, with the result that neither are satisfied.

These plants have a strong rootstock that grows within the gravel and throws off many runners. To propagate, the root-

Cryptocoryne blasii

This plant originates from Thailand and has crinkled, broad ovate leaves, the underside of which are deep reddish-brown. Dislikes strong light and prefers slightly acid water.

stock of large plants can be split up, or the new plants provided by the runners, can be replanted.

C. beckettii

Found naturally in Ceylon, *C. beckettii* is one of the smallest of the family, its leaves, a delicate green, are elongated and pointed, and tend to grow in a horizontal position giving the plant a somewhat untidy appearance.

It prefers soft water, but will thrive in moderately hard water. Grow to about 6 inches.

C. cordata

The leaf form of this species is similar in shape to *C. griffithii*. The large, broad leaves are somewhat heart-shaped near the base and slightly pointed at the tip, they are a rich dark green in colour, and sometimes the underside of the leaves are reddish brown. The veining is well marked.

It grows to an average height of 10 inches. Remember that these plants are naturally tropical and should be maintained at a temperature ranging between 70°-80°F (21°-26°C) Reproduces by runners.

Cryptocoryne nevillii

This is another very small species, the leaves are slightly arched and lanceolate in shape, their colour ranges from light to dark green. This species should not be shaded too much by other plants. Propagation as the other *cryptocorynes*.

C. griffithii

C. griffithii is a native of Indonesia and Malaya. The leaves are dark green in colour with a reddish underside and they

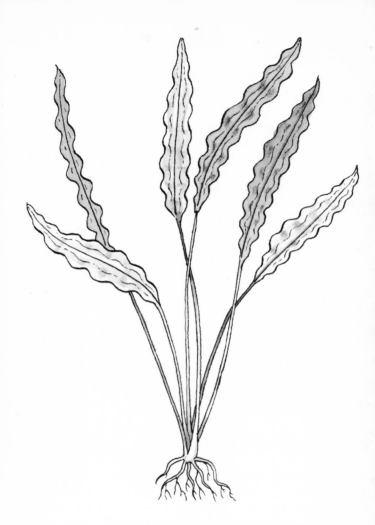

Cryptocoryne undulata

In many respects this species is very similar to *C. Willisii*, and indeed it may well be a variety of this species. It is an excellent aquarium plant, that prospers best in well illuminated tanks.

Cryptocoryne willisii

The leaves of this plant are brown green in colour and wavy. Unfortunately it rarely flowers in the aquarium, but it is a beautiful plant for using as a focal point from which to plan the balance of the aquarium scene (see text).

have somewhat crinkly appearance. This species is extremely similar to *C. cordata* and can easily be mistaken for it identification can be established by the more rounded lea tip and tougher leaves.

It is a robust species, that will stand considerable rough handling and knocking by the net.

Reproduction by runners.

C. willisii

This is probably the most popular of the *Cryptocorynes* The leaves are a bright medium green and have a wavy edge Propagation is by means of a short runner, or by splitting of a part of the parent plant. Once this species has become established in an aquarium, they should not be removed unnecessarily as they have an objection to new locations.

They grow to about 6 inches in length.

The young plants can then be collected and planted where required. If the plants are allowed to remain on the surface they will surely die, but take a comparatively long time to do so.

Echinodorus brevipedicellatum (Narrow Leaf Amazon Sword Plant)

This beautiful plant from Brazil is shown to its best advantage in large aquaria. The shortish stems are between 2 and 6 inches long topped by long, narrow, lance-like leaves. In natural waters the plant will grow well above the surface, but in the aquarium they tend to lay flat along the surface.

Propagates by runners and is best maintained at a tem perature around 70°F (21°C). Cooler water tends to keep the plants small, and less robust.

Echinodorus berteroi

Commonly known as the Cellophane Plant, *E. berteroi* is one of the most attractive aquarium plants, the delicate, thin, membranous leaves float on the end of long thin stalks. It grows best at a temperature of about 75°F (24°C) without too much light.

Echinodorus longistylus
This is an ideal plant for large ornamental tanks. It can be used to form backgrounds, planted in groups, or used as focal plant to accent a particular feature of the general layout (see text).

Cryptocoryne blassii

Cryptocoryne nevillii
(Normal form)

Cryptocoryne nevillii
(Pigmy form)

Echinodorus paniculatus

Echinodorus longistylus (Long-Shafted Sword)

E. longistylus is a swamp plant found naturally in Brazil, It is ideally suited to large aquaria, but the plant has a tendency to grow above the surface of the water. Its shape is typical of the genus with long elliptical leaves about 7 to 9 inches in length on stalks that can reach up to 20 inches high.

It likes a water temperature of about 75°F (24°C) during the summer, and a few degrees less during the winter, and water a little soft. Natural sunlight will help to provide robust specimen.

Propagation in an aquarium is not easily achieved, but which can be separated, and planted out.

Echinodorus martii

Found naturally in Brazil, this species is a relatively newcomer to the aquarium. It has lanceolate leaves, varying in length between 12 and 20 inches, with slightly wavy edges and rounded tips. The stalks are extremely short — only about 3 inches long. It is a plant that enjoys the higher temperature range of 75°-85°F (24°-29°C) and soft water, and should only be considered for very large aquaria.

Reproduction by runners, which should be pressed down into the sand where the new plants begin to develop.

Echinodorus paniculatus (Giant Amazon Sword)

This plant has a wide range over South America. It is the largest of the Sword plants with leaves attaining a length of 20 inches, the shape of the leaves is typically lance-like, tapering both ends to a point, and running down the stalk towards the root.

Because of its large size, *E. paniculatus* needs a large aquarium, it also requires reasonably soft water, and a

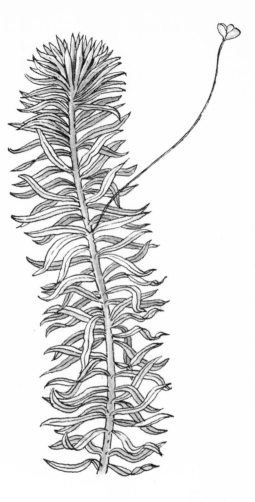

Egeria densa

A useful aquarium plant because of its fast growth rate. *E. densa* has no special requirements in respect of planting media, but grows best in hard water with good illumination (see text).

regular daily supply of either sunlight or artificial light. Temperature around 75°F (24°C) is ideal, lower temperatures tend to restrict the growth of the plant.

Reproduces by runners which should be pressed down into the sand where the new plants begin to develop.

Egeria densa (Argentina Anacaris)

Previously known as *Elodea densa,* this plant is found naturally in sub-tropical South America. It is a beautiful plant with densely clustered leaves set closely to a central stem. The roots are sparse and consequently do not anchor very well into the gravel, a little lead may be necessary when first planted, they have the advantage however, of drawing their nourishment from the water, so they can be cultivated free-floating. The colour of *E. densa* is a fresh green, and one of its main attractions is that it is a quick growing plant — a growth of one inch a day not being unusual, the closely packed leaves offer a hideout to young fish, but they are too coarse for spawning tropical fish.

Early aquarists considered this plant to be one of the best oxygenators, undoubtedly it is a good oxygenator, but by present day standards, it is not considered so highly, however, do not exclude it from your selection on that account, as it makes an interesting specimen, if only for its speed of growth.

Eichhornia crassipes (Water Hyacinth)

E. callitrichoides and *E. canadensis* are two species that are restricted to the outdoors pool or cold water aquarium, and normally *E. densa* is only suitable for cold water, but it has been used quite successfully in tropical tanks. *E. densa var crispa* however is suitable for either, the leaves and stem are shaped the same as *E. densa,* except that they bend back upon themselves and form a curly pattern.

This water Hyacinth is a beautiful and interesting plant, but it is not considered so in its natural habitat. It is found in

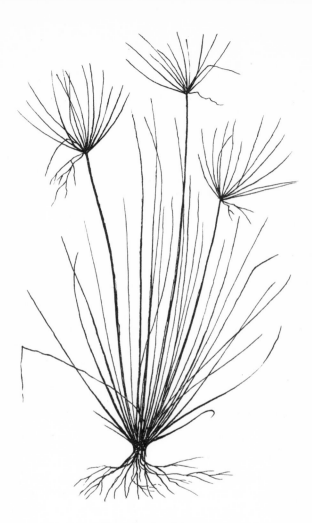

Eleocharis vivipara

Eleochares vivipara is a pretty, grass-like plant that has grown very popular among aquarists. Its popular name, Umbrella Plant, is derived from the new plant growths which resemble the spokes of an umbrella. Best results are obtained by adjusting the light source, not too bright, or too dark.

most tropical regions of the world where it grows along the banks of rivers and other waters, and floating in dense matts, it grows so rapidly and densely that navigational problems are caused to boats using the waters.

The leaves are a shiny light green and spray outward on short stem to form a rosette. The base of the stems are somewhat swollen and contain a sponge-like substance which gives the plant buoyancy and keeps it afloat.

The roots, blackish-blue in colour are long, dense and bushy, and make an ideal spawning refuge for fish that spawn adhesive eggs near the water surface.

The flower, which grows on a stalk from the centre of the rosette, is a delicate blue or violet.

Although this plant has been used in the aquarium for many years, it is not an easy plant to grow, because of its height above the water surface it is necessary to reduce the water level. The Water Hyacinth needs plenty of light, and moist warm air which makes it more suitable for the swamp aquaria or aquaria that have an extensioned glass top to contain the warm moist air. It usually dies in winter unless kept in a tropical greenhouse.

Elatine macropoda (Big Footed Elatine)

Found naturally in Southern Europe and North Africa, this plant does not seem to be very readily obtainable in the United Kingdom, this may well be because the plant prefers temperatures just below 70°F which is a little cool for the average tropical aquarium.

The small leaves, about $\frac{1}{2}$ inch long and $\frac{1}{8}$ inch wide have rounded tips and are attached in little bunches to a horizontal stem from which the root filament grows down into the gravel.

When first planted they should be left undisturbed for a period until they become firmly established and specially guarded from the attention of inquisitive fish who will disturb the water surrounding them.

Propagates by division of the stem and roots.

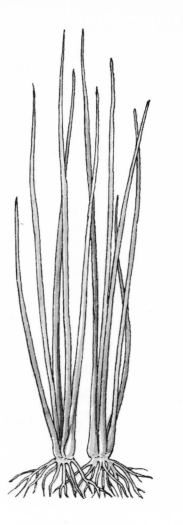

Heleocharis acicularis

This is an accommodating plant that will thrive in both warm and cold water aquaria. It does, however, require plenty of light. Also known as Nilegrass (see text).

Heleocharis acicularis (Needle Grass)

H. acicularis is widely distributed all over Europe. North and South America, Asia and Australia, where it grows along the edges of stagnant waters.

The leaves are thin, similar to the stiff blades of some grasses, and like grass the leaves sprout directly from the root-stock stemless. The roots spread out from plant to plant similar to the runners of *Valisneria,* the filaments burrowing down below each plant. In ideal conditions the plant will spread to form a matt which covers the whole floor of the aquarium. Dense patches make ideal spawning plants, the fine needle like blades give excellent protection to eggs scattered by egg laying fish. Temperature requirement for tropical aquaria should not be lower than 75°F (24°C) Propagates by division of the rootstock.

Heteranthera zosteraefolia

This plant is found naturally in Brazil and Bolivia. In some respects it resembles *Anacharis.* The pale opaque green leaves are attached in alternative positions on a somewhat brittle stem. It prospers best in well-lit aquarium, with the water at a temperature of about 70°F (21°C). It is a hardy plant, with the advantage of growing quickly.

Hydrocleis nymphoides (Water Poppy)

Found naturally in the tropical regions of South America the Water Poppy is a pretty addition to the aquarium with its shiny green heart shaped leaves floating on the surface of the water.

It is not a particularly difficult plant to grow in the aquarium providing the conditions are favourable, that is plenty of sun-light, if not a source of strong artificial light. The plant also seems to prefer soft water. Propagation is by shoots which sprouts from the nodes of the stem.

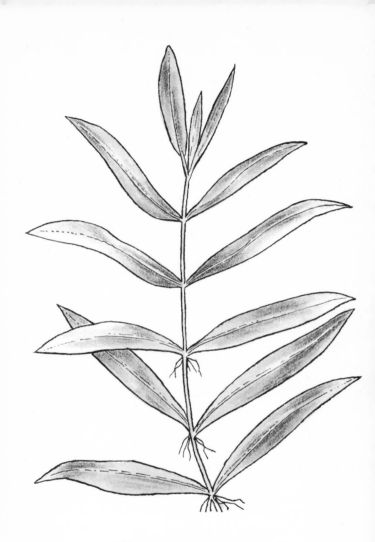

Hygrophila angustifolia

Isoetes echinospora

This is a beautiful green plant, unfortunately only suitable for the cold water aquarium. It cannot be grown successfully in temperatures higher than 50°F (10°C). Leaves easily damaged.

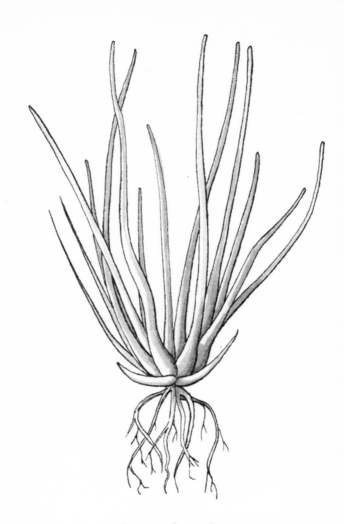

Isoetes lacustris

Similar to *I. achinospora* in that it can only be grown in cold water aquaria. It nevertheless is much easier to cultivate in not too hard a water. Leaves are brittle and should be handled with care.

Hygrophila polysperm (Water Star)

This species is found naturally in the shallow waters of S.E. Asia, and it is one of the easiest of plants to grow. It has all the appearance of a terrestrial plant and it is interesting, because it is the only aquatic in the genus. The leaves sprout from a central stem in opposed pairs, their shape being not unlike those of the antirrhinum, they are a pretty light green in colour.

Reproduction is achieved by cuttings snipped off just below a node with outgrowing root tendrils on the stem. It does require plenty of light and will thrive abundantly in temperatures between 70° — 80°F (21°—26°C).

Isoetes setacea (Quiltwort)

Found naturally in Southern Europe, *I. setacea* is a suitable plant for mid positions in the aquarium. The pale green, slim, rush-like leaves generate direct from the compact rootstock and may reach a length of 12 inches. Their tendency to flow upwards in slightly wavy vertical lines makes the plant ideal for forming curtains of green tracery.

It is a hardy species suitable for relatively high temperatures, but it does grow rather slowly.

Propagates from spores encased in capsules situated at the base of the leaves. Young plants will often shoot up from around the base of the older, established plants.

There are other species of *Isoetes,* but these are not suitable for the general requirements of the tropical aquariums.

Lemna gibba (Duckweed)

This species is found naturally in Europe, Asia and Africa, and is a common sight around the edges of our ponds and lakes, forming a green mantle which from a distance is easily mistaken for scum.

The dainty little leaves only about $\frac{1}{8}$ inch long, are dark

Lagenandra lancifolia

This plant, originating in India and Ceylon, is sometimes found in aquaria. In appearance, it is very similar to the *Cryptocorynes*, but it is inferior to these for aquarium use.

Lobelia cardinalis

An excellent plant for the tropical aquarium, if given good illumination and a loam and gravel soil. If it should flower they will be a beautiful flaming red.

green and shiny, and a quantity of these makes a rather pretty roof to an aquarium in which it is being used to cut down light. Surprisingly the addition of this plant to an aquarium does not seem to impair the surface of the water from absorbing oxygen from the atmosphere. Reproduces by budding, resulting in chains of little plants.

L. minor (Small Duckweed)

A slightly smaller species than *L. gibba.*

L. triscula

The pale green leaves of this species are quite different in shape from the usual Duckweeds, they are connected in little triangular columns.

Limnobium stoloniferum (South American Frogbit)

Found naturally in the tropical regions of South America, *L. stoloniferum* is a beautiful floating plant with attractive heart shaped leaves attached to a central root by short stems, forming a rosette pattern. The leaves are sponge-like which gives the plant buoyancy. Long, thread-like roots hang down into the water.

This plant likes plenty of light, but if this is too intense, the leaves are likely to turn brown. Like most tropical swamp plants they require a moist warm atmosphere, consequently, the aquarium should be covered, but it will be necessary to lower the water to provide adequate space for the plant above the water level, alternatively, a special glass cover can be added to the top of the aquarium to increase the air space.

L. stoloniferum prefers soft water and a temperature around 75°F (24°C) or slightly higher.

Propagates by shoots from the parent plant.

Ludwigia natans

A truly ornamental plant that grows rapidly and robustly when given the correct amount of light. Found naturally in Tropical America (see text).

Limnophila sessiliflora

L. sessiliflora is found naturally in S.E. Asia and parts of tropical Africa and Australia. It is a similar plant to Cabomba consequently the two are sometimes confused. The main difference is in the shape of the leaf. When viewing *Cabomba* from above the fan-like leaves form a semi-circle, but the leaves of *L. sessiliflora* viewed from the same position, form a complete circle. The arrangement of the leaves are bunched rather close together making it an ideal spawning plant.

This species will not thrive unless it is supplied with plenty of light, natural or artificial, and a water temperature no lower than 68°F (20°C).

The fine feathered leaves are particularly susceptible to the settling of mulm stirred up by fish and air-lifts, it clogs the fine interstices and caused the plants to die.

There are about thirty known species of *Limnophilia,* but only two are currently being used by aquarists in addition to the above *L. gratioloides* and *L. heterophylla.*

Propagates by cuttings. Smallish shoots snipped off from where they join the main stem make the best plants.

Ludwigia natans (Floating Lugwigia)

This plant is found in the Southern regions of the U.S.A. The leaves are lance-shape and pointed at both ends. They are joined to the main stem in pairs opposite each other. Their colour is a brownish green, sometimes brilliant red on the underside. *L. natans* requires plenty of light, if you plant them in a shady part of the aquarium the leaves are likely to droop.

It is not a very difficult plant to propagate which is accomplished by snicking off a piece of plant just where the leaves join the stem, where you can see the young tendrils shooting, the cuttings can then be planted in the usual way.

L. atternifolia is a species not really suitable for tropical aquaria, the leaves are attached to the main stem alternatively instead of directly opposed as in *L. natans.*

L. palustris is the only European species.

Eleocharis acicularis

Ludwigia natans

Myriophyllum brasiliense

Nomaphila stricta

Marsilea drummondii

This is not a particularly easy plant to cultivate, although some aquarists do so successfully. It originates in Central and South Australia in silty soil. Requires a controlled amount of illumination best ascertained empirically.

Lysimachia nummularia (Moneywort)

This pretty little plant is found naturally in Europe. E. Asia and North America. The light green rounded leaves are attached to a central stem in opposed pairs. It is a hardy plant with strong decorative appeal.

L. nummularia is not difficult to grow providing adequate lighting is supplied and it will certainly benefit from occasional exposure to sunlight.

Najas microdon (Nymph Worts)

Found naturally in America, this plant is a vivid green in colour, with narrow generally opposed leaves which sit on the stems in much the same manner as the leaves of carnations. Occasionally fine indentations will be found on the edges of the leaves.

N. microdon is a fast growing species, providing they are given plenty of light and warmth, the temperature of the water should never be allowed to drop below 70°F (21°C). Given these conditions, they will grow into dense clumps useful for spawning fish that lay their eggs in thickets.

Propagation is by cuttings. The cuttings should be planted so that the gravel just covers the first two leaf position, they will then root quickly.

This plant is very similar in appearance to *Elodea callitrichoides,* but as this is a cold water species, the warmth of a tropical tank would soon kill it.

N. minor is a smaller species, but it is unsuitable for the aquarium.

Myriophyllum (Water Milfoil)

This genus of plants have a delicate fern-like beauty with fine abundant leaves attached to a central stem that make them ideal spawning plants. The plants will float naturally just below the surface and in aquariums where the water depth

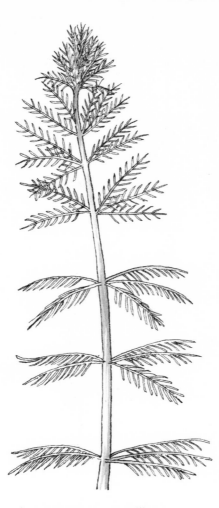

Myriophyllum brasiliense

Commonly known as Parrots Feather, this plant will grow successfully in most tropical aquaria, but the leaves should not be allowed to grow above the water surface, otherwise the submerged leaves will deteriorate, and drop off (see text).

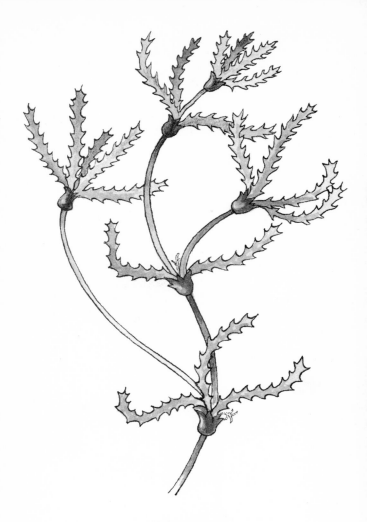

Najas marina

This is not a particularly good plant for the aquarium. It is found naturally in fresh to brackish water.

Nitella flexis

This has many advantages as an aquarium plant. It is attractive, grows readily from any piece stuck into the planting medium, and makes an excellent breeding plant, its close network of stems and leaves forming a natural egg trap (see text).

has been reduced, give excellent protection to livebearer fry, If the plant is used to catch the eggs of spawning fish, they should be planted in thick clusters.

When planting, the stems should be stripped clean of leaves for about 2 inches from the bottom, and pressed into sand.

Myriophyllum does not like very warm water, most species should be maintained in aquaria with a water temperature no higher than 75°F (24°C). Although a hardy plant, it requires constant attention. If it is to prosper, mulm deposited on the leaves by water disturbances should be removed, similarly mulm collected around the roots should be syphoned off.

Propagates by cuttings.

M. alterniflorum

This is a British species.

M. brasiliense

is found in South and Southern America, it is a deep green colour with distinctly separated feathery leaves forming a shape like a snow crystal star when viewed from above. Suitable fortropical freshwater aquariums.

Nitella flexis

This species is found all over Europe, North America and Asia. It is a particularly dainty plant. The leaves, more like small stems from which flowers have been removed, are divided into two or three extensions at the tips positioned radially around the main stems. Leaves and stems are dark green.

These plants have thread-like roots which are insufficient to anchor the plant when first planted therefore, a temporary method of anchoring is necessary.

N. flexis requires plenty of light, but if this is excessive they tend to become inundated with algae. Apart from its decora-ative appeal, it is a useful plant for the breeding tank. The

Ottelia alismoides

This is not an easy plant to cultivate. It requires soft clear water, and a planting media containing loam and peat. The leaves are very pale green, and the general shape of the plant is truly ornamental. Requires a warm environment about 77°F (25°C).

Pistia stratiotes

This is a beautiful floating plant that unfortunately does not prosper very well in aquaria because of the large amount of foliage above the water surface requiring space and air (see text).

long tendril-like stems can be anchored along the floor of the aquarium to form a dense mat for protecting the eggs of spawning fish and young fry.

N. gracilus is another similar species.

Nomaphila stricta (Giant Indian Water Star)

This is a swamp plant from S.E. Asia where it is found naturally in very shallow water and along the shore. The top of the plant protrudes well above the water surface. In many respects it is similar to *Hygrophilia polysperma,* the stems are strong and the leaves a beautiful vivid green, a little paler in shade on the underside, and somewhat varied in both shape and size, they are pointed at the base and the tip, and grow up to 5 inches in length. It is not unusual for fine hairs to grow on the stems and leaves.

N. stricta prefers a temperature around 75°F (24°C) and softish water.

Propagates by cuttings from the stems of strong plants, or even leaves. It is a plant that thrives best under the influence of strong light.

Pistia stratiotes (Water Lettuce)

This interesting species of floating plant range over most of the tropical and sub-tropical regions of the world.

The leaves cascade from a central base like the petals of a flower and are light green in colour, fluted and velvety. Under suitable conditions, the plant will reach a diameter of 4 inches.

The roots hang down below the plant and are white to blue in colour, and although they are fine and bushy, they are not really dense enough to provide a spawning ground for surface egg layers.

This species does not prosper well in the aquarium, the raised top covers with built in lights are not ideal because they tend to dry the leaves which then go white.

Potamogeton coloratus

A widely distributed plant found in Europe, Australia, Algeria and the W. Indies. It is a good plant for the tropical aquarium if it can receive a regular supply of daylight.

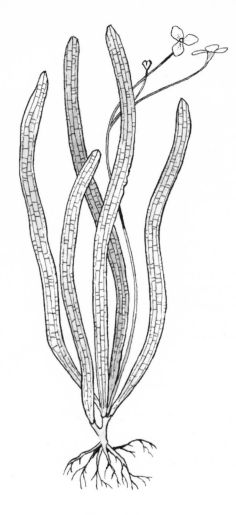

Sagittaria natans

This plant is found naturally in N. Europe, more suited to unheated tanks (see text).

Propagation by surface runners, preferably in shallow water.

Riccia fluitans (Crystalwort)

This pretty floating plant is found naturally all over Europe, America and Asia. In the aquarium it forms a tangled matt of interlocking fibrous-looking greenery, sometimes to a thickness of $\frac{3}{4}$ inch. The small leaves are pronged and shaped like the minute antlers of a deer.

Riccia should not be allowed to grow too thickly, otherwise light and free passage of water will become restricted and decay will set in. Due also to the close packed formation of the leaves, it is difficult to keep it clean of algae, but an abundance of snails will help to keep it clean. However, care should be taken to exclude any Ramshorn snails, they will simply make a meal of it.

It is a really good oxygenator that multiplies by separation, one part separates from the parent and becomes a parent itself and so on.

It requires plenty of light, but not so near that the leaves become burnt.

Sagittaria (Arrowhead)

Sagittaria is a genus of plants that closely resembles *Vallisneria.* The plant leaves irrespective of the species, are shaped more or less in the form of an arrowhead, hence its name *Sagittaria* after the mythical heavenly archer.

S. natans

Found naturally in Northern Europe, this vivid green species with ribbon-like leaves is only rarely found in tropical aquaria because of its dislike of warm water. It is a moderately sized plant well suited to tanks about 12 inches deep. The leaves usually reach 6 to 9 inches.

Propagates by runners.

Sagittaria montevidensis

This is a South American plant that is often used in the tropical aquarium but it is not one of the best plants for this application. Can be grown from seed.

S. subulata

Found naturally in the eastern regions of the U.S.A. this species could easily be confused with *Vallisneria spirallis,* the differences being mainly in the leaf structure, the leaves are narrow and ribbon-like, terminating in a tapering point, their colour being somewhat darker than *S. natans.*

S. lorata

Found naturally in the N.E. regions of U.S.A. this species may well be known by other specific names of *S. eatonii, pusilla,* or *gracilis.* It is a hardy plant, with vividly green leaves, ribbon-shaped, sometimes broadening at the tips.

S. gigantea

This species is as its name suggests a much larger species averaging a length of 15 inches, with leaves $\frac{1}{2}$ inch or more in width. When well rooted, they are sturdy and will stand quite a lot of knocking from the net.

There are other species of *Sagittaria* that are more fitting for the cold water and aquaria, consequently they have been omitted.

All the above species reproduce by runners, but it has been observed that *Vallisneria* and *Sagittaria* rarely do well if planted in the same tank.

Salvinia auriculata (Small Eared Salvina)

Found naturally in stagnant waters of Tropical South America, *S. auriculate* is one of the most interesting and prettiest of the floating plants available for tropical aquaria. The small hairy oval leaves are attached in opposed pairs to a common stem, and where they join the stem, root-like appendages hang down into the water. These brown, feathery threads are not true roots, but leaves that have become modified and adapted to absorbing the necessary nutrients from the water. Spore capsules sometimes develop at the base of the submerged leaves, but little is known about their development at the present time.

Because *salvinias* natural habitat is still water, it thrives very well in the aquarium, but it does require plenty of strong light and a temperature range between 64°F—77°F (18°—25°C). It does not take kindly to drips of water from the cover glass, therefore, the cover of aquaria containing *Salvinia* should be tilted.

Multiplication is effected by sprouting, and under favourable conditions it will grow profusely. Aquaria sited in a greenhouse, and subjected to a reasonable amount of sunlight, are particularly suited to rapid growth. In natural conditions, the plant prefers shallow water containing decaying plant matter and infusoria, the clear water of the aquarium does not compare with these conditions, but it will still prosper although the leaves are likely to be smaller.

Salvinia is a plant that must be used with a little discretion, as a thick layer on the water surface shades the plants below from the available light source. On the other hand, it is an ideal plant for providing a refuge for small fry, and other tiny water creatures. It is also an ideal plant for the breeding tank, for fish that spawn near the surface. Bubble nesters frequently make use of this plant to reinforce their nest of bubbles.

Salvinia is described under many different names, but these are often no more than colour varieties.

S. natans is a species found in Europe, North Africa and Asia Minor, but it is not recommended for use in the aquaria.

Sertularia cupressina (Sea Cypress)

Sea Cypress is not a plant, but its usefulness in the aquarium justifies its inclusion. Sea cypress is in fact, the external skeleton of a hydroid polyp. It is found naturally in the tidal waters of Holland, Germany, Iceland and Great Britain and along the coasts of the North Sea. It grows on the sea bed, sometimes in bunches or beds up to 10 inches in

Spirodela polyrhiza

This small floating plant has oval leaves with a dark green surface and a reddish-brown on the undersides. It thrives in cold tanks but does not do well in heated aquaria.

Vallisneria spiralis

Sagittaria subulata

Synnema triflorum

Commonly known as Water Wistera, this is a fast growing plant useful for establishing new tanks. It is not fussy about planting media, and propagates readily from cuttings (see text).

81

depth, and in its natural state it has a delicate mossy appearance. The 'plant' consists of a skeleton made of chitin — the same substance that forms the outer case of insects. The tiny inhabitants of this skeleton are removed by a process of washing and drying, which leaves it clean and more or less dehydrated. It is in this form that it is available to aquarist. When dropped into water the fronds spread out to make a real life-like leathery plant.

If a single feather is viewed under a low powered microscope, the little pockets that once housed the tiny polyp can be seen quite clearly.

Although basically used as a decorative piece, its real value lies in its use as a breeding refuge.

When used in the breeding tank it is unnecessary to cover the floor of the aquarium with sand. The Cypress can be weighted with small pieces of lead attached to the base, the buoyant stems will then float vertically, making an ideal egg trap, or refuge for young livebearers.

Another advantage of Sea Cypress is the fact that it can be stored dry, preferably in a plastic bag for safety, and will last indefinitely if carefully handled.

After being used in the breeding tank, it can either be washed gently under a running tap and returned to the aquarium or thoroughly dried and stored.

Synnema triflorum

This attractive plant, sometimes described as Wisteria, normally ranges throughout S.A. Asia, where it is found in tropical swamps, paddy fields and along the banks of rivers and lakes.

It is closely related to *Hygrophila,* with a strong vertical stem which can reach about 14 inches in height, the short leaves are light green on the upper surfaces and a whitish green on the underside. The irregularly shaped, lightly indented, leaves grow from the stem in such a way that when viewed from above they form beautiful rosettes.

Stems and leaves are covered with short hairs.

Propagates by cuttings which grow roots quickly. It does not like very hard water, but does need plenty of light and temperature around 75°F (24°C).

Utricularia exoleta (Bladderwort)

This species is found naturally in S.E. Europe, Africa and Australia. It looks like a tangled mass of light green cotton with little knots attached to the strands, as if someone had tried to untangle it and lost patience. The little knot-like appendages are little bladders through which the plant feeds in an unusual way.

The bladder, called utricles, are in fact traps for catching the prey on which the plant draws its nutrient. The bladders are equipped with a tiny trap door that is normally closed, and when the prey — small micro animals, infusoria etc. — comes in contact the door flies open and the inrush of water carries the prey inside to be digested. This plant is ideal for spawning surface egg layers and as a protective maze for very young livebearers, being of a closer formation than Riccia.

When using Bladderwort it is advisable not to have other floating plants in the same tank, as they come hopelessly entangled with each other.

U. exoleta grows best in softish water and in a temperature no lower than about 70°F (21°C). Propagation takes place by fragmentation of the plant which only requires to be put in water to grow new shoots.

U. vulgaris is another species but it is not suited to the warm temperatures of the tropical aquarium.

Vallisneria (Eel Grass)

Vallisneria is a genus of perennial water plants belonging to the family of the Frog Bits. It is distributed naturally over wide areas of the tropics sub-tropics and the warmer parts of the world.

They are ideal furnishing plants for the aquarium with their light-green leaves and tall grass like blades. They are

Vallisneria spiralis formatorti folia

A beautiful grass-like brilliant green plant. Grows to a height of 12″. Propagation is by runners. It will not thrive in very strong or very weak light but prefers a soft light.

hardy plants useful for forming backgrounds, and need no special attention except a reasonable amount of light.

They propagate by shooting out runners, the baby plants setting themselves. Female flowers grow on thin, spiral stems which reach up to the surface. Male flowers form at the base of the leaves, detach themselves and float on the surface to join the females.

Vallisneria spiralis (Common Eel Grass)

The shape of *V. spiralis* is typically grass-like and has the advantage of being an excellent oxygenator. It is a tall plant with leaves that rise vertically from the crown to the top of the water, where they float along the surface.

Vallisneria gigantea. (Giant Eel Grass)

As its name suggests, this is a somewhat larger species, the leaves may well reach 5ft in length, and widths in excess of one inch. They are found naturally in New Guinea and the Philippines.

Vallisneria spiralis - forma tortifolia

This is a corkscrew variety of *V. spiralis* with spirally wound leaves and it does not grow quite so large. They are hardy but tend to remain small with less pronounced corkscrewing if maintained in water too cool.

Index